KT-117-539

LIVING IN TIMES PAST

CONTENTS

MOONLIGHT PUBLISHING

Prehistoric people made stone tools and weapons.

The first creatures who walked upright and looked a little like human beings had appeared on Earth by at least 3 million years ago. They are known as hominids.
As thousands of years passed, these beings evolved and spread out across the world.

What did prehistoric people look like?

Archaeologists, who study the way of life, or civilization, of people who lived in the past, have found many prehistoric skeletons. These show how humans changed over time. It seems that 100,000 years ago there were people who looked like us. They could make a sharp cutting edge by hitting one stone against another. The period when stone tools were used is called the Stone Age.

Tools used to work leather: knife, scraper, hole-punch and bone needle.

They had spears, arrow-heads and scrapers for cleaning animal skins. With needles made from bits of bones, they stitched together simple garments of skins and furs. Until 10,000 years ago Europe was covered by glaciers for long periods and it was freezing cold. Prehistoric people needed to wrap up warmly. Their new skills helped them to survive the Ice Age.

They were excellent hunters as well as skilful artists.

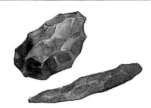

They made fire by striking a flint against a stone...

...or by rubbing two pieces of wood together.

The stick has to turn in the piece of wood...

...very fast to produce enough heat.

<u>These people followed herds of grazing animals to hunt them.</u>
<u>They were nomads.</u>
They set up makeshift camps in quiet spots. Their shelters, made of bones, stones, branches and anything else they could find, were adapted to the climate and the place where they stopped. They also used caves and rock shelters. People ate bear, deer and even mammoth meat. They stole birds' eggs, caught fresh fish, picked plants and berries and dug up roots and tubers. When they learnt to make fire they began to cook their food, rather than just eat it raw. And a fire lit at night scared away wild animals.

<u>Archaeologists have found paintings in caves dating back to prehistoric times.</u>
Early people made paints by crushing coloured rocks and mixing the powders with animal fats. They drew the animals they hunted on the walls of caves. The paintings may have been meant to bring good luck to the hunters. You can visit some of these caves today. Clay figures of women from around the same time have been found, as well as animals carved on pieces of rock or bone.

People began to build villages and rear animals.

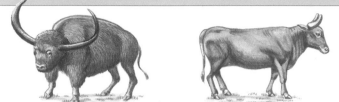

The cow's ancestor, the aurochs, was a fierce animal.

Wild boars became pigs and wild sheep today's sheep.

As the Ice Age came to an end, the glaciers melted and the weather slowly warmed up.

Aurochs, wild boar and wild sheep appeared. Some tribes realized that by breeding animals and penning them in they could tame them. Then they wouldn't have to hunt for meat anymore.

The beginnings of farming

Our ancestors learned to collect seeds from wild plants. They sowed them and waited patiently for them to grow. When the plants were ripe they were harvested. People no longer had to search far and wide for vegetables and fruit.

Now people could stay in one place. With their stone axes they made clearings in the forest to plant crops and graze animals. They built villages, and silos to store the tribe's grain through the winter.

Tools made of stone, wood and metal

Fighting broke out more often.

Sometimes raiders plundered the tribe's food stores; or two tribes fought over a particular area of land which was more fertile than another, or which had a constant supply of water. These differences could easily lead to full-scale war. The chieftain led his people into battle. When he died he was buried in a tomb with all his jewels and weapons.

All sorts of crafts developed.

People needed furniture, pots, jewellery… They learnt to forge metals, to spin wool, weave cloth, work clay and carve wood.

They ploughed the fields and forged metal in fire.

The first looms were laid flat on the ground or against a wall. Women wove wool and linen to make clothes for their whole family.

People made huge stone circles, perhaps in honour of their gods.

The Iron Age

By 1000 B.C. the Hittite peoples of the Middle East had begun to use furnaces to extract iron from iron-ore. Much lighter and easier to work than bronze, iron soon took over as the main metal used. It is very strong and remains sharp longer than bronze. It is still one of our most important metals.

Spinning and weaving were invented.

People began to collect wool. By rolling it between their fingers and pulling it out into strands, women were able to spin long threads. These could be interwoven to produce pieces of cloth which would be stitched together to make a garment.

Pottery vase

As weaving techniques improved people were gradually able to produce finer cloth of better quality. Whole pieces of cloth were treated with plant and flower dyes to produce brightly-coloured textiles.

The Bronze Age

By mixing together copper and tin a new metal was produced: bronze. From about 3000 B.C., this was the most commonly used metal. Bronze tools were strong and could be forged into all sorts of shapes. Improved tools helped craftspeople make better equipment. Carpentry developed and looms were perfected.

Pieces of iron-ore were thrown into a furnace which was kept very hot. The metal formed a lump which fell to the bottom of the furnace, while the waste materials ran out.

The mighty Nile flows through the desert of eastern Africa.

About 4000 B.C. the first settlements were built on the shores of the Nile. Time passed and villages grew into towns. By 3100 B.C., the country was united into the Kingdoms of Upper and Lower Egypt and ruled over by a king, known as the Pharaoh. The ancient Egyptians were a learned people whose magnificent monuments, temples and palaces can still be visited today.

AFRICA

Nile

Along the banks of the Nile it is cool and there is plenty of water for the crops.

In the summer, the sun is so hot everything seems to burn up. Then suddenly, every year, the snows melt on the mountains far away and water rushes down from the hills, making the Nile swell and overflow its banks. After three months the river goes down again. The mud and silt that it carried are left behind in the valley to form a rich layer of earth.

Children's toy

Hunters used a weapon very much like a boomerang to catch wild geese and ducks.

Along its banks lived the ancient Egyptians.

The Egyptians loved family life.

They particularly liked playing games together: dice, knuckle bones and a game like snakes and ladders, which they called senet. Rich Egyptians organized splendid feasts for their friends, with an orchestra, or dancers, to amuse the guests. The musicians played harps, lutes and flutes, while the singers beat time with small rattles, called sistras.

Mirror

Make-up spoon

What did the Egyptians wear?

The men wore skirts or loincloths while the women wore long dresses of fine linen. Children usually didn't wear any clothes at all.

Men often shaved their heads and faces. Most wore skull caps, while the rich nobles wore heavy wigs. The women grew their hair long, although they also often had wigs. Their wigs were longer than the men's and might have coloured beads braided into them.

Houses were built of bricks

and painted bright colours. People sat out on the flat roofs in the cool of the evenings. The rich had beautiful gardens, with sycamores and papyrus growing round a pool.

Dancers and a musician

The peasants used a shadoof to carry water from the river to the fields. The bucket was hung on one end of a pole and balanced by a weight at the other end.

Their king was called the Pharaoh.

The Pharaoh had many slaves to wait on him.

Friendly neighbouring peoples sent gifts to the Pharaoh.

He ordered palaces, tombs and temples to be built.

He enjoyed going lion-hunting in his chariot.

The Pharaoh's army was huge and well-trained.

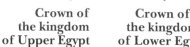

| Crown of the kingdom of Upper Egypt | Crown of the kingdom of Lower Egypt | Pharaoh's crown of united Upper and Lower Egypt. |

The Egyptians believed that the Pharaoh was the son of Ra, the sun god.

Huge statues of him stood outside the temples. He was shown wearing a headcloth, called a nemes, over his wig and a false beard on his chin. On his forehead was a small model cobra, a uraeus, which was thought to protect him from evil.
As the ruler of both kingdoms of Egypt, the Pharaoh wore the double crown.

The scribes helped the Pharaoh rule.

Scribes could read and write. These were rare skills in those days, so the scribes were very important. They kept the country's accounts on rolls of papyrus, a sort of paper made from the stem of the reed with the same name. They checked the harvests and the building of the temples for the Pharaoh, making sure his orders were carried out.

The Pharaoh wearing his kepresh, the blue crown.

The queen

The prince carries a lotus flower, symbol of rebirth.

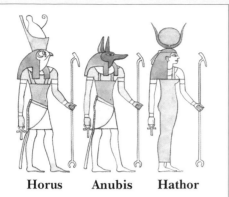

Horus   Anubis   Hathor

Who are these figures with animal heads and strange crowns?

They are the gods who watched over the Egyptians. Often they were half human and half animal. Horus, god of the sky, had a falcon's head. He was the son of Isis and Osiris, the gods of fertility. Jackal-headed Anubis was god of the dead, while Hathor was goddess of love and music. The Egyptians had many more gods. Every god had his own great temple. Nobody was allowed in, except the priests. The statue of the god was in the most secret room of the temple. Sometimes, on feast days, the statues of the gods were carried out and the priests and people walked with them in long processions.

Archaeologists have explored the pyramids.

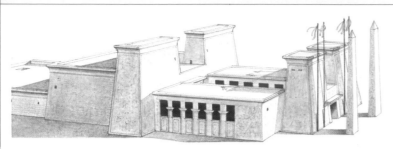

The two enormous stone needles standing at the entrance to the temple are called obelisks.

The Egyptian pyramids are gigantic tombs which stand in the desert, out of reach of the Nile's flood.

Inside each one there is a maze of secret galleries leading to the room where the Pharaoh's mummy lies hidden. Other rooms are filled with furniture, vases and jewels. The pyramids were designed to make it almost impossible to get inside once the Pharaoh had been buried.

A pyramid could take thirty years to complete.

First the stone had to be fetched. Some kinds of stone could be found in the desert close by, others, like granite, were ordered from distant quarries. The stone was loaded on to boats and floated down the Nile. Then it was dragged on rollers to the place where the pyramid would be built.

Some of the blocks of stone weighed over 20 tonnes. As they didn't have cranes, the Egyptians made huge ramps of brick all around the pyramid. The stones were pushed on rollers all the way to the top. Thousands of labourers worked on the site.

By patiently clearing away the sand, archaeologists have found statues, furniture, pottery, paintings and even temples.

Inside the pyramids they found the mummies of the Pharaohs.

When somebody died, the body was embalmed, to keep it from rotting away. A body preserved like this is called a mummy.

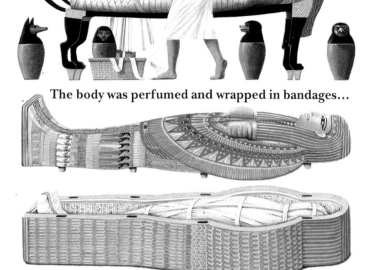

The body was perfumed and wrapped in bandages…

… and the mummy was placed inside a beautiful wooden coffin.

The ancient Egyptians believed there was a new life after death.

They would enjoy it only if their bodies did not decay. Even poor people, whose tombs were cut out of the mountainsides, were embalmed. Food and furniture were placed in every tomb, as well as statues of slaves, to serve the dead in their new lives.

The dead bodies were carried across the Nile to the burial ground.

The pyramids of Cheops, Khephren and Mykerinus

Grave-robbers often broke into the pyramids to steal the treasures.

That's why the entrance was sealed and hidden and the galleries were all blocked off.

The highest Egyptian pyramid is the tomb of Cheops: it is 146 metres high.

Pyramid of Cheops:
1. King's chamber
2. Store-room
3. Unfinished chamber
4. Great gallery

Ancient Greece was made up of rival city-states.

Greece is set under a luminous sky in the sparkling Mediterranean Sea. Greek civilization was at its height about 2,500 years ago.

Although the people spoke the same language and worshipped similar gods, they did not feel part of one country. Greece was split into many city-states, prosperous towns which ruled over the surrounding countryside and villages. Each city-state had its own rulers, its own army and its own customs. Athens and Sparta were two of the most powerful.

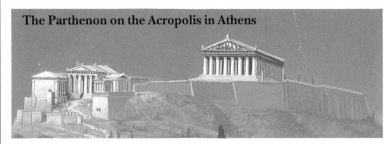
The Parthenon on the Acropolis in Athens

On the Acropolis, the 'High City', the Athenians built their temples. When they were destroyed by the Persians in 480 B.C., they rebuilt them, more beautiful than before. The most imposing was the Parthenon, the temple of the goddess Athena, protectress of the city and goddess of war, wisdom and the arts.

Every male citizen served in the army.

The different states were often engaged in war against one another, though they did unite against common enemies, such as the Persians.

On this map of the Mediterranean coastline the shaded areas show where the Greeks settled and founded colonies.

Sparta

Athens

The gods were central to Greek life.

They had to be kept happy with gifts, or offerings, which could range from a chicken to an ox. The animal was sacrificed to the god; its throat was cut open on the altar by a priest.

The Greeks also consulted oracles.

Dionysus,
god of wine

Aphrodite,
goddess of love

The temples took many years to build.

Architects drew up plans for what the finished building should look like. Hundreds of workers cut the marble blocks, shaped them and polished them. The columns were left white, drawing the eye up towards the brilliantly-coloured carvings of gods and heroes that decorated the top. They glimmered and glistened in the sunshine and could be seen from miles around.

These three typical Greek columns of different periods (Doric, Ionic, Corinthian) are still copied by architects today.

The Greeks exercised their bodies and educated their minds.

Everyone went to the theatre, even prisoners!

Poor people didn't have to pay anything. Lots of plays were performed, one after another, all day long from sunrise to sunset. They were put on in honour of the god Dionysus, near whose temple the theatres usually stood.

Comedies were cheerful plays which made the audience laugh, while tragedies showed the difficulties and sorrows of life.

The writer of the best poem won an ivy crown.

The actors wore masks: smiling ones for comedies, sad ones for tragedies.

The theatres were open-air and the audience sat on steps around the stage. Many of these theatres are still in use.

The Greeks believed that physical exercise was an important part of education.

Boys had to start exercising when they were very young. They were sent to a palaestra, or wrestling-school, where they practised in a cool shady courtyard surrounded by colonnades. Musicians gave them the beat and their teachers guided their movements with sticks, which they also used to separate the wrestlers when there was a foul.

Only in Sparta, Athens' main rival, did the girls do as much sport as the boys.

When boys turned 18 they were allowed to exercise in the men's gymnasium,

Strigil and oil container

a public sports complex, often outside the city walls. In these pleasant surroundings men met to talk as well as to wrestle. Philosophers, Greek scholars and teachers met and had discussions with their pupils after the training sessions.

Wrestlers oiled their bodies. They used a strigil to scrape off the sand and sweat which clung to their skin after a fight.

They organized the first Olympic games.

1

2

3

4

Olympic sports:
1. There were races for runners dressed in full armour.
2. Boxers had their hands wrapped in strips of leather.
3. Throwing the javelin
4. Discus throwers hurled flat discs of stone that were extremely heavy.

Athletic competitions were held throughout the year, and were usually part of a religious festival. Athletes from rival cities competed against each other.

Long jumpers held weights in their hands to give them greater impetus, so that they could go further.

The most famous of all the games were those held at Olympia.

They took place every four years and lasted seven days. Our modern Olympic Games are copied from those started in Greece thousands of years ago.

Boys took part in the games too.

They had special events in which they competed against each other. They weren't allowed to box or to join in the most violent kind of fight, the pankration. The fighters were forbidden to bite each other, to stick their fingers in each other's eyes, or to break each other's fingers – but pretty well everything else was allowed!

The Games held at Olympia were part of a festival dedicated to Zeus. While they were taking place, all wars and disputes between the states were interrupted.

The Greek way of life was simple.

Greek houses were very plain.

Luxury was kept for temples and public buildings. Houses were built of clay or wood, and plastered and painted over. The walls were very thin, and thieves often broke in. During the hot summer months people slept out of doors, on the flat roofs.

What kind of lives did women lead?

Women from wealthy families led sheltered lives, not going out very much. They spun and made clothes, and managed the household. Slaves and servants did the heavy work: grinding the barley, making the bread and fetching water.

Fine plates and vases for use at banquets

The streets were narrow and crowded.

They weren't paved and there were no gutters, so in wet weather they became muddy, and in hot weather they stank. All the same, they were full of life! Farmers came in from the surrounding countryside to sell pigs, hens, fruit and vegetables. Craftsmen ran stalls selling clay lamps, vases, weapons and armour. Wine-merchants, shoe-makers, rope-makers and fishmongers displayed their wares under coloured awnings and called out to attract their customers' attention.

They were great thinkers and courageous explorers.

The Greeks traded their olives for wheat from the Crimea or Egypt, and Baltic wood...

They planted vines and olive groves in the colonies and brought with them their language, their money and their sciences.

...their grapes and wine for African ivory and for iron and copper from Thrace.

The Greeks invented democracy.

All citizens had equal rights before the law and could have a say in what was best for the city. They voted on important decisions by throwing, or casting, specially-made discs. This practice was unknown anywhere else at this time. But it was a limited kind of democracy: neither women, foreigners, nor slaves were allowed any rights.
Most citizens had at least one slave. These were people who had been taken from defeated cities. They were owned by their masters and could be bought and sold as if they were objects.

The Greek way of life influenced all the peoples of the Mediterranean area with whom they had contact.
Their arts and philosophies spread, and even today many of our beliefs rest on ideas first put forward by the Greeks.

The Greeks explored every corner of the Mediterranean.

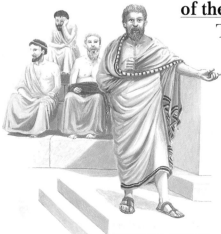

They established colonies in Spain, France and Italy, and around the Black Sea.

Public speakers, or orators, tried to convince listeners that their point of view was the right one.

Rome was at the centre of a vast empire 2,000 years ago.

The city of Rome grew up under the Etruscan kings, and later as a democratic Republic. The city was ruled by a council called the Senate, but all citizens could be involved in government. The Romans were excellent warriors: they took over Italy and went on to conquer lands throughout Europe and the Middle East. Bitter rivalry between Julius Caesar, one of their most brilliant generals, and other leaders, led to civil war and a long period of unrest. In 27 B.C., a powerful general, called Octavian, became the first of a line of emperors.

Roman men went often to the public baths.

They washed and played games and talked with their friends about politics and state affairs. The baths were one of the great pleasures of their lives as they didn't have running water at home.

Later they might go to one of the entertainments organized by the emperor.

The Forum was the main public meeting-place. There were temples and triumphal arches and inscriptions to remind Romans of their famous past. Most of the buildings were made of white marble. Here people voted on the laws and held meetings.

Lavish entertainments were provided for the Romans.

At the theatre,
the public could watch
plays all day long.
Their favourites were
knockabout farces,
and pantomimes with
music and songs.

A theatre

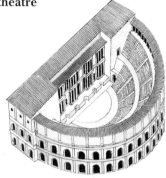

**At the circus the games
went on for days and days.**
The seats were free,
but people spent
a lot of money betting.
There were often
animal fights: a bear
might be pitted
against a bull,
or an elephant
against a rhinoceros.
Gladiators fought
against bulls, lions,
panthers, tigers...
The cruellest fights
were those between
gladiators. Some were
professional fighters,
others were slaves and
condemned criminals,
or poor people
attracted by the chance
of high wages.

The streets of Rome were noisy and full of life.

Roman scales

What a din!
At night, you could hear carts rumbling along the road, and the drivers swearing at their animals. During the day, crowds pushed and bustled through the streets. The roads were dirty with the rubbish people threw out of the windows. Poor people lived in tenement blocks that were up to six or seven storeys high. They weren't very well made and often collapsed or caught fire.

Off to school
Only rich boys, between the ages of seven and fifteen, went to school. They set off very early in the morning, with a slave to carry their wax tablets and the sharp stylus which they used to write with. Their teacher was often a Greek; he would punish bad students with a rod, called a ferula.

What games did Roman children play?
They had toys such as hoops, wooden tops, and dolls made of wax or clay. They played at jacks and had many board games.

Slaves (1, 2) with the master and mistress of the house (3, 4)

1   2   3   4

How did the Romans dress?
Everybody wore the basic tunic: slaves had a knee-length one, while other people could afford longer ones made of finer material. Wealthy citizens, especially men, draped a large semi-circular piece of cloth, called a toga, over their tunics when they went out.

At the barber's, men were shaved and scented.

They drank wine with friends in the taverns.

The Romans borrowed their gods from the Greeks.

The Romans worshipped many gods.

They even honoured their emperors. But their main gods were much like those of the Greeks. Jupiter was the father of the gods and was similar to the Greek Zeus. Like the Greeks, the Romans too performed sacrifices. After the Emperor Constantine became a Christian in 312 A.D., this new religion became the most popular in the empire.

A Roman at home

The prosperous Roman, whose house you see here, woke at dawn and had a light breakfast of bread and cheese. Then the day's business would be taken care of. The main meal of the day, the cena, was eaten in the middle of the afternoon. It might be boiled ostrich, spiced hedgehog and fried roses! Poor Romans ate simple meals of bread, olives, grapes and honey.

Every house had an altar.

Every morning slaves dressed the lady of the house.

The master gave his day's orders to his slaves and servants.

The cena was eaten lying on a couch.

School was a room, shut off from the street by a curtain.

How to wear a toga

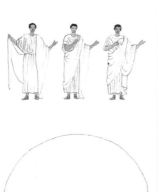

25

The Roman legions were a conquering force...

The Roman legions formed a huge army.

There were 310,000 soldiers during the reign of the Emperor Augustus (27 B.C.-A.D. 14). The army was divided into legions, each with 6,000 soldiers. They were all issued with standard equipment and were trained to fight in formation. To protect their new territories, the soldiers were made to build fortified camps at the boundaries. A huge network of roads was created, so that the army could travel quickly.

The Romans improved upon the siege techniques they learnt from the Greeks.

A boat harboured at Ostia, Rome's port on the mouth of the Tiber. Roman trading-ships sailed to every port of the Mediterranean.

In the countryside around Rome, lots of people were hard at work.

There were slaves working for their masters and farmers working their own lands. They grew vines for grapes and wine, harvested olives and pressed them to make a rich oil. The Romans used a lot of oil and didn't make any butter. They didn't keep cows, but had herds of goats and sheep for milk.

A simple wooden plough pulled by oxen was used to prepare the soil for sowing. Here and there, amongst the vines and cypress trees stood the holiday villas of wealthy Roman families. These were beautiful country houses, with gardens and courtyards. They were the ideal place to escape the noise of the city and the heat of the southern summers.

Carts weren't much good for transporting things. Whether they had two wheels or four, they were slow, bumpy and expensive to run.

Most goods travelled by sea in huge merchant-ships. Wrecks of Roman vessels have been found carrying over 10,000 amphorae (earthen-ware containers) on board.

Ostia was Rome's main port.

When a ship arrived, its cargo was loaded on to a river-boat which travelled up the Tiber to the warehouses in the city.

You could buy anything in Rome: the whole of the Empire sent its produce to the city to be sold.

glass	pottery	ivory	marble	metals	wood	papyrus
wool	linen	leather	horses	wild animals
oil	wine	fruit	cereals	honey	murex shell

When the harvest was bad cereals were imported from Gaul, Sicily or Egypt and the poorest families in the city were given free grain.

Wherever the Romans went they left traces of their civilization and Roman monuments can be found in many places they settled. This triumphal arch is in Africa, for example.

The Roman empire weakened...

By A.D. 350 Rome had weakened and could no longer defend her territories. Barbarian peoples from outside the empire started moving west looking for land. They were allowed to settle and became Rome's allies. However, they were attracted by the great wealth of the empire: its mighty cities and its huge grain stores. They took up arms and in 410 Rome itself was captured.

Meanwhile, in Asia, a tribe of fierce horsemen called the Huns had been building an empire of their own. These brilliant warriors were feared everywhere they went and they demanded the Romans pay them to spare their lands.

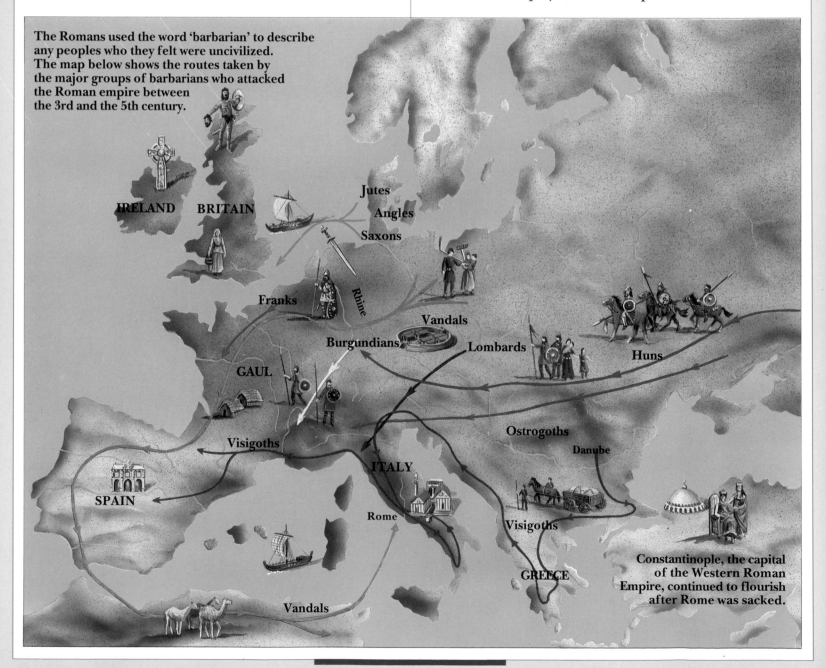

The Romans used the word 'barbarian' to describe any peoples who they felt were uncivilized. The map below shows the routes taken by the major groups of barbarians who attacked the Roman empire between the 3rd and the 5th century.

IRELAND

BRITAIN

Jutes

Angles

Saxons

Franks

Rhine

Vandals

Burgundians

Lombards

Huns

GAUL

Visigoths

Ostrogoths

Danube

ITALY

SPAIN

Rome

Visigoths

GREECE

Constantinople, the capital of the Western Roman Empire, continued to flourish after Rome was sacked.

Vandals

When they were refused payment they began to attack the empire. By 451 they had reached Gaul, now France.

Their king, Attila, was a formidable leader. He led his army as far as Italy before being defeated and forced to retreat.

The Vandals crossed the frozen Rhine on their way to Spain and North Africa.

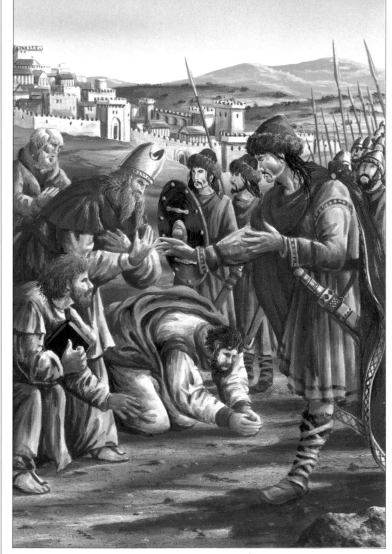

The Bishop of Troyes begged Attila to spare his city. The Huns were only stopped when some of the German barbarian tribes joined forces with the Roman army.

The Roman way of life was slowly forgotten.

In the centuries following the invasions many people in Europe continued to live as they had done under the Romans. But neither the local people nor the barbarian invaders knew how to look after the buildings left by the Romans or maintain the sewers. The roads fell into disrepair and travel became more difficult. Over a few generations much of the knowledge and many of the skills of the Romans were completely lost.

German warriors were fierce men and brave fighters; to them it was an honour to die on the battlefield.

Wonderfully elaborate jewellery was made at this time.

Most people lived by farming.
The barbarian invaders settled in abandoned Roman farmsteads or built new villages. They planted hedges around the fields and sowed vegetables.
They kept large herds of goats and sheep.

God's judgement:

The judges made the accused person walk over burning coals. They were proved innocent only if they weren't too badly burnt.

Battle-leaders and tribal chieftains carved out small kingdoms for themselves.
Their family members, friends and loyal soldiers formed the nobility. They were given land to hold in the king's name, and swore they would supply the king with men and weapons if he ever needed them. The nobles protected their territories from invaders and administered local affairs. They claimed as their own most of the food the peasants grew. This allowed them to pass the time feasting and hunting wild boar, deer and aurochs in the forests.

As the Roman empire declined, trade decreased and many luxury goods were no longer imported.

The Church was an important power in Europe.

Monasteries were founded where monks lived, prayed and worked together. Some dedicated monks became missionaries; they believed they should spread Christianity amongst the barbarians to convert them. They were largely successful and Christianity became

Europe's main religion.

In Gaul the powerful Frankish king Clovis was baptized a Christian with all his warriors. By the 7th century, most of Britain had been converted. Many monasteries were built and Britain became an important centre of religious learning and teaching.

Every church was a sanctuary. This meant that anyone who entered, including criminals, was safe once inside.

The new rulers minted coins just like the Romans had done at the time of the empire.

When Charlemagne, Clovis' grandson, was made Holy Roman Emperor in 800, he was crowned by Pope Leo III, head of the whole Church. By doing this the Pope showed that God and the Church accepted Charlemagne as emperor. Over time it became usual for kings to be crowned in church by an important official.

Soon it became hard to tell a barbarian and a Roman citizen apart. Charlemagne's empire stretched from Spain across Germany.

The emperor was a learned man who encouraged the arts and Europe was united under the protection of the Church. But this happy state of affairs did not last. In the 8th century more invaders began to appear.

An ancient Arab manuscript. Arabic is read from right to left.

A new religion was founded in Arabia: Islam.

Its followers were called Muslims and were led by the prophet Muhammad. After their leader's death in 632, the Muslims began to invade neighbouring countries to convert them to Islam. They were so successful that they forged an empire in the East and in Africa. From there they turned towards Europe. They defeated the Visigoths in Spain and pushed north into Gaul. The Christians all grouped together and managed to stop the Muslims. They expelled them from most of Europe, but part of Spain remained an Arab colony for another 600 years.

Moorish (Muslim) window

Arab doctors, astronomers and mathematicians were very learned: they still had the knowledge of the ancient Greeks and Egyptians. In Europe, Arab – or Moorish – culture brought a new breath of life.

...and Vikings from the north.

The Vikings came from Scandinavia. They had fast longboats which were easy to steer and were powered by sails or oars. **Around 790, they began raiding the wealthy coastal monasteries of Ireland and Britain.**

They were excellent sailors and travelled as far as Russia and round southern Spain into the Mediterranean. They were looking for farming land, which was scarce in their own countries, and they often married abroad, settling down in their wives' countries.

They established themselves in Normandy, eastern England and central Russia. They were converted to Christianity and soon merged into the local populations. Their most important colony was to be a small duchy in northern France, which became known as Normandy. The Normans followed in their ancestors' footsteps, and sailed the seas looking for land and plunder.

Charlemagne

People were terrified of these invaders who came from the sea. A large raiding band might have up to 400 men, although usually they came in groups of about 60. They wanted money and valuable goods as well as land.

The Middle Ages was the time of the great castles.

Castles remind us of a time when life was much more dangerous than today, with bands of thieves and outlaws, wild animals and, all too often, war. The lords of the land fought against each other constantly, and the king was powerless to stop them.

Though most are now in ruins, castles were strong and formidable in their day, and cleverly built.

Castles were first built over a thousand years ago. They began by being simple wooden towers with a ditch around them. They could be easily burnt down.

Wooden castle

By the end of the 11th century, some castles were built of stone. The walls were up to 8 metres thick.

Building a castle could take forty years. No two were entirely alike, but they all had ramparts, a drawbridge and a strong tower, called a keep.

Each castle was built in a spot that could be easily defended. Often this was on the banks of a river or the top of a hill or crag. Enemies could be seen coming from a long way away off and the soldiers had time to get ready.

While the castle was being built, a village for the workmen grew up around the walls.

You can still find remains of these castles all over Europe: in France and Britain, Spain, Italy, Switzerland and Germany...

1. Ditch or moat
2. Ramparts
3. Battlements
4. Crenellations
5. Wall walk
6. Arrow slit
7. Portcullis
8. Drawbridge
9. Curtain wall protecting the keep
10. Machicolations through which stones and boiling oil could be dropped on the enemy
11. Keep

Reconstruction of
a 14th century castle

The lord and his family lived in the keep.

There were often feasts at the castle.
What were the guests served to eat?
It could be roast boar, eel pie, venison,
chunks of bread and spicy sauces.
And perhaps, if it was a special occasion,
a roast peacock. For dessert there might be
tarts and puddings made with cream and
honey. There was ale, cider and spiced
wine to drink. On the table were pottery
bowls and goblets made of pewter.
The more important guests would often
be served on gold and silver tableware.

The feasting went on through the night.
Jugglers and acrobats, dancing bears and
monkeys entertained the guests.
Travelling musicians, called minstrels,
were hired to play music
to dance to, and
troubadours sang songs
of love and bravery.
In the kitchen
the servants
were kept busy till after
the last guest had gone to bed.

Knife, forks, and a hunk of bread for a plate

The lord loved hunting and having tournaments.

How did the lords hunt?

They reared and trained falcons.

The bird flew up, spotted a rabbit, dived down on to it and flew back to the lord's gloved hand.

The lord hunted for fun, but also to provide food for his table and to kill any animals which might harm his sheep or damage his crops.

After being a page, a young boy became a squire, a servant to a knight. **At eighteen, he would be blessed in church and made a knight.** On that day he received a horse and a sword from the lord he promised to serve.

Tournaments were often held, in which knights met to prove their strength and courage. Some champions went from castle to castle, challenging others. Their names and exploits were known to everyone. The winner received a prize from the noblest lady present.

The peasants worked for the lord and paid for his protection.

How did the people live?
In the village each family had one room which they shared with their animals. As soon as winter was over, the peasants were out working in the fields. They sowed the grain, sheared the sheep and harvested the crops. They foraged for nuts, mushrooms and berries in the forests.

Trees were felled to make clearings in the forests in which to plant crops.

The lord owned the land around the castle and all the people who lived there.
Each family received a house and some land to grow their own crops, but in return they had to work the lord's land. They also had to give him a part of their harvest and a number of their animals. They had to look after the ditches and paths, repair the castle ramparts and chop wood. For a fee they could grind their wheat in the lord's mill, bake their bread in his oven and make their wine in his wine press. During times of war the villagers were allowed to shelter inside the castle walls with all their animals.

The peasants' life was hard. They weren't allowed to hunt wild animals and often didn't have enough food to last them through the winter.

Everyone had to pay the lord a tax, or toll, to use his bridges and roads.

The Church was another powerful landowner.

The lord's word was law.

If you annoyed him you could end up in the dungeons. Sometimes people were put in the stocks as punishment. They were fastened by their hands or feet and couldn't duck the rotten vegetables or stones that people threw at them.

Wine press   Oven

What did the lady of the castle do?

She looked after the household and was in charge of all affairs if the lord, her husband, was away. She was responsible for making sure there were enough provisions and for organizing meals. She taught her daughters to weave and to perform other household tasks. If anyone was sick she nursed them back to health using her knowledge of herbs.

Little girls were engaged to be married very young. They often became wives at fifteen. Boys left their mother even earlier. At eight they were sent to a neighbouring castle to be a page and learn to ride and fight.

In the Middle Ages books were rare and precious. They were written by hand and decorated by the monks.

Abbeys and monasteries, with their splendid libraries, became important centres of learning. The Church was wealthy and powerful at this time, and had its own law courts and law enforcers.

This made it important for the king to have the Church's support.

He got it by giving land and money. Instead of living simply, praying and teaching the word of God, many bishops and high officials of the Church built splendid palaces and lived in great comfort.

In the towns lived merchants and craftspeople.

Townspeople were free.
Surrounded by high walls and fortified gates, towns looked like enormous strong castles.
The merchants and craftspeople who flocked to the towns didn't have to pay taxes to the local lord. They could hire soldiers to protect them against robbers and other armies.
Townspeople got their groceries and meat from shops.

Other goods and luxuries were supplied by the workshops of weavers, smiths, potters – craftspeople and artisans of all kinds. As they grew richer merchants and craftspeople banded together in guilds and companies. As a group they could be nearly as powerful as the lords and the bishops and were able to stand up against them if necessary.

The cathedral was the bishop's church.
It was usually in a large, important town from which the bishop controlled all the other priests in the area.
The church was a central part of town life and as people grew richer, they began to spend money on improving it. Towns competed to have the most beautiful church and many huge cathedrals were built throughout Europe. Famous architects were invited to draw up the plans and hundreds of craftspeople helped to decorate the building with statues and carvings and stained-glass windows.

The farmers around towns had better tools and horses, which they bought from the merchants.

Cathedrals were built and universities founded.

The cathedral square was one of the liveliest places in the city.

Travelling actors perfomed plays there and pedlars displayed their goods before the townspeople. Friends met in the square to talk and sermons or proclamations from the king would be read out to the townspeople. The market was also held here. From the square led off narrow, winding streets full of shops. Often all the people working in one trade had shops in the same street or area of the town.

The Church ran most of the schools.

That's why they were near the cathedral buildings.
There, taught by their master, young boys learned Latin, music, grammar, arithmetic and astronomy. Girls didn't go to school at all.

In the 12th century, the first universities began to appear. The University of Oxford, one of the oldest in Europe, started as a series of separate colleges, each set up by wealthy men.
When their studies were over, the students relaxed in the taverns. They drank, talked and sang songs. The evenings often ended up in a drunken brawl on the streets!

Most people's houses were built of wood.

On the ground floor there was a shop or workshop opening on to the street, a warehouse or sometimes a stable. The two rooms on each floor above were the family's living quarters.
The streets were narrow and only very rarely cobbled. When it rained, people sank up to their ankles in mud!

The Renaissance was a period of change and rebirth.

By the 15th century life in Europe changed. Explorers set off on dangerous voyages, returning with all sorts of new goods. Printing and gunpowder were two of many important inventions. The Renaissance had begun. This word means 'rebirth' in French. It was an age of discovery and technical development.

In the 1440s Johannes Gutenberg invented a printing press which used small movable lead letters. Letters were positioned to make up words on the page. A series of pages could be printed quickly. The Arabs introduced into Europe paper, which they made from rags. Thanks to printing, books became much cheaper.

Cannon on wheels

New lands were discovered and sea-routes opened.

Astrolabe

The spices and silks made in the Far East were in great demand in Europe.

These goods were brought overland to Europe by Arab merchants who prospered from this trade. Helped by improved ships and maps, Europeans were able to find their own sea-route to the East. The Portuguese, Dutch and British all reached India, the East Indies and China by sailing round Africa. Merchants returned bringing boatloads of goods.

Spices for example, were used in Europe both as flavourings and to cover the taste of rotting food. Each trip took up to three years and was very dangerous. The sailors often got scurvy, from lack of fresh fruit and vegetables. The few who survived were lucky to escape shipwreck!

Travelling west to the Indies, explorers found a new land they named America, with its enormous gold and silver reserves. They brought back potatoes, chocolate, and other new foods. Many Europeans went to live in America. Their newly invented cannons and muskets helped them overpower the local people.

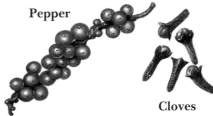

Pepper

Cloves

Italy became the centre for the arts.

Statue of a discus thrower

The Italian city-states became rich thanks to trade with the Far East.

They were ruled by powerful families, or dynasties, wealthy enough to lend money to kings and popes. Many had made their money through trade and were clever bankers. They invented the bill of exchange, which was like a modern cheque, so that merchants didn't have to lug sacks of gold around with them, and be easy prey to highwaymen or bandits. These Italian princes of the Renaissance built themselves beautiful palaces and dressed extravagantly. They wore silk hose, or tights, and short velvet jackets. They saw themselves as learned men and surrounded themselves with artists and musicians.

In Florence, Lorenzo de Medici, who was called the Magnificent, lived at the centre of a refined court. He was a poet and scholar as well as a ruler. He encouraged scientists, astronomers and philosophers as well as many famous artists of the time.

Greek and Roman art and learning became a fashionable area of study.

People were interested in archaeology and began to collect Greek or Roman statues and pottery.
Ancient books were found lying forgotten in dusty libraries. They were translated into Italian and other modern languages. More people could read now and, as printing developed, books became affordable. Poets and philosophers began to use their own languages, rather than Latin, so that a wider audience could appreciate their work.

Science and technology blossomed too.

Design for
a flying machine

Leonardo's diagram
links the human body
to the square
and the circle.

Leonardo da Vinci was the ideal Renaissance genius.

He was a great artist and could paint, draw, sculpt and write poetry. At the same time, he was a skilled engineer, capable of diverting a river or building fortified ramparts. He designed machines to comb wool, to look at the stars, even to fly... Like most artists of his time, he travelled from court to court, selling his skills to the princes and kings of Europe.

Leonardo da Vinci

Copernicus

In every country doctors, mathematicians and astronomers made new discoveries. People had believed that the Earth was at the centre of the universe since the time of Ptolemy, an Egyptian astronomer. In Poland, in 1543, an astronomer called Nicolaus Copernicus (1473-1543) proved that it is actually the Earth which revolves around the Sun. The Church banned his findings.

The solar system
according to Ptolemy

The solar system
according to Copernicus

Louis XIV lived at the centre of a splendid court...

Since the barbarian invasions, Europe had been ruled by powerful kings who passed on their power from father to son. They governed alone, advised only by a council of ministers and were seen to be directly responsible for the well-being of their people. Amongst these rulers, Louis XIV of France (1638-1715) was the most formidable. He personally approved any decision concerning the country. He said of himself: 'I am the State'.

<u>Louis XIV was known as the 'Sun King'</u> because he made himself the shining centre of his court. About 10,000 people lived at the palace, many of them nobles who were paying their respects to the king.

Louis dressed in the height of fashion, wearing make-up, a long, curly wig and high-heeled shoes. Each evening he chose favourite nobles to help him get ready for bed.

An army of servants looked after the needs of the court.

Nothing was too good for the King.

Louis ordered a magnificent palace to be built for him at Versailles, outside Paris. Over three thousand labourers worked on it for twenty-five years. When finished it was declared the most grandiose palace in Europe and its style was immediately copied by other kings and nobles. The best artists decorated the rooms. The walls were of coloured marble and on the ceilings were painted pictures showing the King's bravery and strength. Long colonnades and many mirrors gave the impression the palace was even bigger than it actually was. But many of the bedrooms, even those where the royal family slept, were dark and dingy. There was no running water so it was impossible to have a bath. Most people didn't wash, they just sprayed themselves with lots of perfume!

17th century fashion accessories

After discussing business with his ministers, the King relaxed in the gardens.

The grounds of the palace were laid out in vast lawns. Neat paths, bordered by clipped hedges, led to ornamental ponds in the distance, where fountains splashed. This sort of garden had never been seen before, but it became a great success throughout Europe. Parties and banquets were held in the gardens. There were displays of fireworks and performances by the best dancers, musicians and actors.

Outside the palace walls, what was ordinary life like?

This young musician is the 8-year-old Mozart (1756–91). He was a child prodigy who performed for many of the kings of Europe.

All the European royal families lived in great wealth and splendour. But the French court remained the most magnificent, even after the death of Louis XIV. New fashions in clothing, furniture and art spread from Versailles to the courts of other nations.

The luxurious life-style of the kings and their court was supported by taxes from the poor. In cities throughout Europe people lived in terrible conditions. Their houses were small and cramped. Water had to be drawn from the well or the river, and was often polluted by all the rubbish that was dumped in it. All sorts of diseases were passed round and few babies lived past the age of twelve months. Food was expensive and even a loaf of bread cost as much as a man could earn from a hard day's work.

The 18th century is known as the Age of Reason.

In the 18th century a movement known as the Enlightenment took shape. Common beliefs in every area of human life were questioned and the powers of the Church and the king were challenged. The population of every country was growing, but there were neither enough jobs nor enough food to go round. Famines occurred and led to rioting in many cities.

In the past the Church had taught that everyone had their place in society and nothing could change that. Now the printing press had made books cheaper and many more people could read. New ideas about freedom and change spread quickly, and more and more people began to speak out against the traditional privileges of the nobility and the Church.

L'Encyclopédie

Denis Diderot (1713-84) and a number of other French philosophers, put together the first encyclopaedia in 1751. They hoped to gather and describe all areas of human knowledge and show how they were related to each other. The first volume was packed with new ideas and was immediately banned by the king. But lots of people rushed to buy it, wanting to learn all they could about the latest developments in mathematics, geography, philosophy and the sciences.

Captain Cook's voyages opened the way to the settlement of Australia by Europeans.

The plantations of America were run entirely on slave labour.

On the west coast of Africa, traders exchanged glass beads and rifles for slaves, whom they sold to the plantation owners when they reached America. During the journey, the Africans were kept in the dark, damp hold of the ship. They were given hardly any food and many of them died. When they arrived at their destination their lives barely improved.

The French scientist, Parmentier, convinced people that this strange vegetable, the potato, was good to eat.

They were beaten and forced to work extremely hard, both in the fields and in the plantation owners' homes.

Most people couldn't see that slavery was wrong. Even the philosophers weren't interested in freedom for everybody.

Europeans had colonies in America, India, Africa... Their plantations, worked by slaves, produced all sorts of new goods. Tea, coffee and chocolate, for example, became favourite drinks in European society and merchants made fortunes from this trade.

In France, the king Louis XVI – descendant of the Sun King – had run up huge debts. When he increased taxation the people rioted. So in 1789 he called the Estates General, a sort of parliament, to help him. Their answer was to proclaim themselves a revolutionary government: the National Assembly. The king was later beheaded together with many of his nobles.

The Declaration of the Rights of Man, made by the Assembly of 1789, was based on the American Constitution (1788) and was itself copied by governments in other countries.

14 July 1789. The fortress of the Bastille, symbol of royal power, was stormed and taken by the people of Paris.

The new constitution declared that all men are born free and are equal before the law. Freedom of the press and voting were introduced. Yet women and poor people were still not allowed to vote.

In revolutionary Europe, scientists were encouraged to experiment.

The first bicycle was invented in Paris in 1790. You had to push yourself along with your feet.

For the first time scientists were encouraged to expand their knowledge.

There were advances in agriculture, astronomy and the other sciences.

All sorts of new machines and gadgets date from this period. In 1790 the first dental drill was produced. The telegraph, a system of transmitting messages very quickly across long distances, was developed. In 1792 William Murdock installed coal-gas lighting in his home. He soon proved its usefulness for offices and factories.

'One king, one law; one weight, one measure!'

This is what the French people called for at the beginning of the Revolution. Till that time measurements had varied from area to area. They could easily be tampered with and people were often cheated when they bought goods. A new measurement was needed, which would be common to all.

1 metre = 10 decimetres = 100 centimetres
The metric system has become the method of measurement almost everywhere in the world. 1 litre, a measure of volume, is contained by a cube with sides of 1 decimetre. 1 kilogramme is equal to the weight of 1 litre of water.

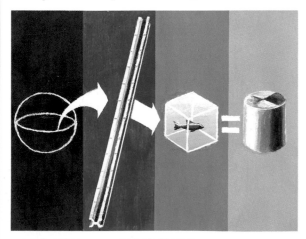

The meridians are imaginary lines over the surface of the Earth, linking the north and south poles.

Scientists decided to find a measurement which could not be altered, a measurement based on the Earth itself.

They divided the length of the meridian by 40,000,000 and in 1799, after years of calculations, came up with the standard metre. The metre is the basis of the metric system.

Scientists invented special instruments to calculate distance, using the known mathematical laws of triangles.

America was inhabited long before any Europeans arrived.

When Christopher Columbus reached the coast of America he believed that he had reached the spice islands of the East Indies. He called the people living there Indians.

These American Indians lived all over the vast continent, on the plains and in the forests, in the mountains and the deserts. Each tribe had adapted to the area it lived in and spoke its own language and had its own customs and way of life.

Bead-embroidered moccasins

The women prepared the food, made the clothes and put up and took down the teepees.

Each hunter, or warrior, could have several wives, and usually had many children. The girls stayed in the village, where they played and helped their mothers. The boys were taught to hunt with a bow and arrow and waited eagerly for the day when their fathers would give them their first pony and take them hunting.

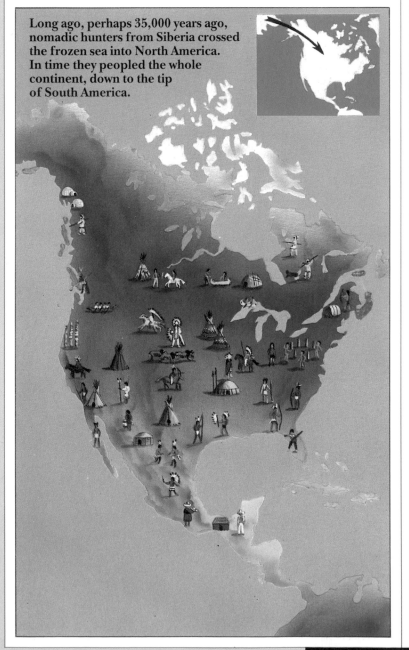

Long ago, perhaps 35,000 years ago, nomadic hunters from Siberia crossed the frozen sea into North America. In time they peopled the whole continent, down to the tip of South America.

The settlers claimed more and more land for themselves.

The Mayflower, the Pilgrim Fathers' ship

Trappers traded with the Indians.

Everything, for the native Americans, was linked to their religion.

To be a hunter or warrior it was not enough to know how to ride and shoot. Warriors had to be initiated and taught the ways of their tribe.

Indians believed that stones, plants, animals and people were all the children of one great spirit, which the Algonquins called the Great Manitou. This meant that everything that existed deserved equal respect. Before hunting the bison that roamed the plains, for example, the tribe danced to ask the animal's spirit forgiveness for killing it.

Many Europeans sailed to America to seek their fortune and live in freedom.

The Indians were quite prepared to share their land with the newcomers.

But they were forced to move and promised lands in the West. They were never given their new territories and finally rebelled. They fought bitterly for their survival, but thousands died in the struggle.

Pioneers travelled west across the prairies.

Wagons, roll!
As more and more newcomers arrived in America, the eastern coast became crowded. Some families decided to travel west, to find land where they could settle and farm.

The pioneers had heavy wooden wagons, pulled by mules or oxen, in which they carried all their belongings and any tools they might need.
The journey took from five to six months and led them across vast, dry plains and over the Rocky Mountains.
It was a difficult and dangerous trip.
At their journey's end they hoped to find a plot of land where they could raise crops and animals and bring up their families.

Oregon, at last!
Here there were forests teeming with deer, grizzly bears and wolverines.
Salmon and trout could be fished from the clear streams.
All the pioneers worked together to help each family put up a house before winter arrived. They made cabins of earth or logs with heavy planks for the roof.
Sheets of oiled paper or thin buckskin were the only coverings for the windows.
The men made basic furniture and their wives sewed clothes and furnishings, while the children collected moss to scrunch up into mattresses. Stones had to be cleared from the fields to free the earth for the plough. There was a never-ending round of work to be done!

Oregon City was one of the first towns ever to be built in the West.

Life in the Wild West

In spring, the settlers would see cowboys driving herds of longhorn cattle past.
The cowboys drove the animals from the grasslands in the south up to the rail-heads in the towns. There, they were put on board trains and taken to feed city-dwellers in the East.

The sheriff kept order in the district.

It was a big day for the pioneers when they went into town for a shopping trip.
They dropped into the general store to stock up with provisions. You could get almost anything there, but you didn't buy, you bartered, trading wheat for sugar, for example. The men often stopped at the saloon for a drink and a game of cards.

Gold was found in California in 1848.
Many settlers turned prospectors, and a mad rush for gold began. Towns sprang up around the mines almost overnight. When the gold ran out, everyone moved on.

As more people came west, transport and communications improved.
Stage-coaches began to make regular trips across America and pony express riders carried mail non-stop from city to city.
On 10 May 1869, the first railway line was opened, crossing from east to west.

The invention of the steam-engine changed people's lives.

Steam-powered vehicle

By the 19th century the Industrial Revolution was transforming everyday life. The modern age had begun. In Britain, James Watt developed the steam-engine in 1781, and steam-powered machines were soon introduced in the coal mines. This meant that more coal could be extracted more quickly and cheaply, which in turn enabled the production of iron, and later steel, to increase.

Steam-engines and tractors made farm work easier.

Steam-powered machines revolutionized industry, transport and trade.

Steam-engines were used to mill sugar, roll iron into sheets and grind corn. Steam-hammers and lathes were developed. Factories were able to produce more than ever before.
Steam ships were built which could soon travel much faster than sailing ships. In 1814 George Stephenson invented a steam-powered locomotive. Britain became the first country to have a public rail service when, on 27 September 1825, a train steamed out of Darlington. By the end of the century this new form of travel had become extremely popular.

A ferry crossing the channel in 1816. It had a steam-powered paddle on one side which drove it.

Factories were built everywhere.

A steel town of the 19th century

A steam train carrying sugar cane to the refinery

Farm labourers moved to the cities to work in the many factories that were built.

Their new lives proved to be back-breaking and miserable. Their working day often lasted 16 hours and they were badly paid. Even children minded machines in cotton factories and went down the mines.
The cities had expanded very quickly and houses for the workers were cheaply built. Few had running water or sewers.

People led unhealthy lives.

There were frequent epidemics of cholera, scarlet fever, smallpox and typhoid, which killed thousands of people. Factory workers in the cities couldn't buy fresh vegetables. Their children grew up with bow legs due to rickets, a disease which attacks the bones. It is caused by poor diet and lack of sunshine.

Silk-weavers lived and worked under the same roof. Their looms took up a lot of room and were very noisy.

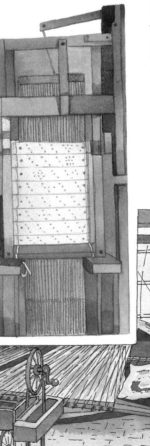

The Jacquard loom used a band of paper punctured with holes to weave complicated designs.

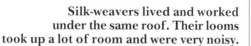

A new metal was developed, called steel.

Steel is a very hard, strong metal,
made from a mixture of iron and carbon. If you look around you'll see lots of things made of steel: car bodies, guttering, tools, pipes… Many objects are made of stainless steel too: chrome and nickel have been added to the steel so that it doesn't rust easily. The steel age started in the 19th century. Huge tall furnaces, called steelworks, were built, where the iron could be heated to very high temperatures to transform it into steel. Many other metals were discovered in the last century too: zinc, uranium and aluminium, for example.

But watch out for toxic waste!
Many metals, such as mercury and uranium, will poison the earth or the sea if we throw them away carelessly. It is important to make sure they are disposed of safely.

Health and home comforts gradually improved.

In the 19th century many European governments began to try to better the lives of the workers and the poor.
New laws limited the hours children and women could work.

By the 1880s many European countries had compulsory free education for all children. Every child had to go to school to learn to read, write and do sums. Exercise was considered a very important part of education too. But despite these improvements in the school system, few girls went to school!

Doctors learnt more about how illnesses are spread by dirt and germs.
In 1858 Louis Pasteur found a rabies vaccine.
He realized that if someone is given a tiny amount of a virus their body learns to fight off the disease: they become immune to it. Other vaccines were introduced, such as the BCG which all children now have to prevent tuberculosis. Surgeons and dentists started to use anaesthetics to put patients to sleep before operations, and antiseptics to help prevent infection.

Oil lamp and electric light

Electricity can be made from water power. ▶

Many towns had electric lighting in the streets. Offices converted from gas to electricity, and machines in factories were electrically powered. Houses became more comfortable: many in western Europe had running water, gas and electricity. In 1876 Alexander Bell made the first telephone: it soon became very popular. All sorts of household gadgets were invented.
In 1884 the first petrol-driven car was produced by Daimler in Germany.
Very soon millions of people were driving and the automobile industry became a force to be reckoned with.

Distance and time are less challenging for us today.

A lighthouse and radar guides ships on once-dangerous night seas.

It's midnight in a European or American city. People are coming out of the cinema; others have stayed at home to watch a tennis match on television, which is being played thousands of kilometres away. Still more have been listening to records, playing computer games or telephoning friends far away. Many others are working in factories, hospitals and airports. Newspapers are being printed and the post is being sorted. Out in the countryside, a farmer is harvesting a huge field on his own with a combine harvester.

Modern technology rules our lives.

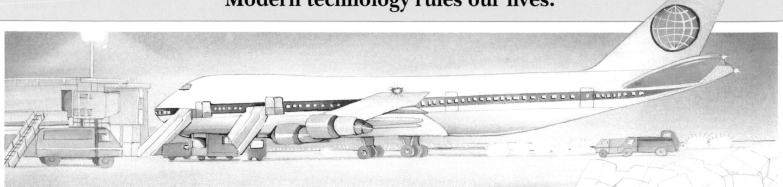

On 20 July 1969 the American astronaut, Neil Armstrong, became the first person to step on the Moon.
Today scientists live in laboratories orbiting the Earth, and we send spaceships to investigate outer space.
Ready-made 'TV dinners' have taken over from traditional home cooking and even our fresh fruit and vegetables come to us from all over the world.
Doctors have found cures for many diseases, and can give you a new heart, liver or kidney, if your own one fails.

But not all progress is good, and some new discoveries may be dangerous both to us and to our environment.
Nuclear energy can be used to produce electricity, but we also make powerful weapons with it which can harm us and our planet.
Let's try and use the wonders of scientific advance to improve the quality of life and to preserve the balance of nature!

Planes take us across the world in a matter of hours.

Crossing borders between countries is easy.

Faxes, telexes and computers send the latest news across the world.

Games and activities,

intriguing facts, a quiz,
sayings, useful
addresses and
places to visit, a glossary,
followed by the index

People lived as nomadic hunters

Cave-paintings

15000 B.C.

Prehistory

People settle in villages and begin raising crops and animals.

10000

We count the years from the date Jesus Christ was born.

In 800, in Charlemagne's reign, the year of Christ's birth was declared the first year A.D. – short for Anno Domini, (meaning 'the year of our Lord' in Latin.) Historians have since found out that Christ was born 4 years before that first year A.D., but it is impossible to change all the dates now!

4000

Writing is invented.

The Pyramids are built.

2500

Ancient history

The Athenians build the Parthenon.

450

The Roman Empire collapses and Europe is invaded by barbarians.

0 ——— **The birth of Jesus Christ**

Muhammad founds Islam.

A.D. 500

Charlemagne establishes his empire.

A.D. 800

The first castles are built.
Norman conquest of England

1000

The Middle Ages

A millenium is 1,000 years.
A century is 100 years.
A decade is 10 years.

Voyages of discovery

1400

Gutenberg develops the printing press.

The Renaissance

1600

1700

The Age of Reason

1800

The Industrial Revolution

1900

Modern times

How do we count the centuries?

Christopher Columbus discovered America in 1492. Is this date in the 14th or the 15th century? It's in the 15th century. But do you know why? Because the 1st century lasted from the year 1 to the year 99. The 2nd century from the year 100 to the year 199, and so on...

Astronomical observatory in Jaipur, India, built in the 18th century ▲

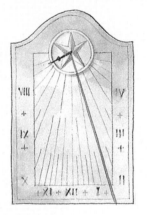

The reason for leap years

A year is actually 365 days, 5 hours, 48 minutes and 46 seconds long. Over a number of years the extra hours add up to make another day. This is why every fourth year we have 29 days in February, instead of 28. Such years are called leap years.

■ Food of the past

Tastes in food have changed a great deal over the centuries. Many of the foods we eat now were not available to our ancestors and they ate foods that we rarely eat today.

Do you think our ancestors would have liked chips and hamburgers for supper?

And do you think you would like the spicy flavours and strong-tasting game, such as pheasant and pigeon, common in the Middle Ages? A typical medieval meal might have been freshwater fish cooked in a wine sauce, washed down with a drink sweetened with honey.

Before fridges were invented, food went rotten if it was kept for too long.

That's why pork and herrings were salted, and ham was smoked: this preserved them. But apples and nuts could keep all through the winter.

No medieval feasts for the peasants!

They usually only had bread and broth, and in winter they sometimes had cauliflower soup or peas and lentils. They didn't know many of the vegetables we now eat everyday.

Potatoes, tomatoes, courgettes, artichokes, oranges, bananas, maize and many other vegetables didn't reach Europe until recently. They were brought back by the merchants who first established trade with the East and the new continent of America.

■ Did you know?

Throughout history people have spent time and effort on the way they look. People like wearing jewellery and dressing in fine clothes.

Prehistoric hunters sewed shells and pearls onto their leather garments, just like American Indians do.

Barbarian tribespeople wore intricately carved and decorated jewellery. Even the fiercest warriors liked to dress beautifully.

Moccasins are the soft, leather slip-on shoes worn by American Indians.

The barbarian peoples, who invaded Europe at the time of the collapse of the Roman empire, wore ornate brooches to fasten their cloaks, and decorated buckles on their belts. The handles of their lethal swords and battle-axes were finely made and beautifully worked.

They were especially proud of their hair. They believed that a warrior's long hair was a sign of his strength.

Under their tunic men wore breeches. These were close-fitting trousers, which they pulled in round their calves and ankles and tied with thick leather or cloth thongs.

The women of the tribe pinned their dresses together with brooches, similar to our safety-pins. Their jewellery was carved with figures of snakes, dragons and other strange animals in intricate patterns.

From head to toe...

In Ancient Greece
all women, except for slaves, wore their hair long. They piled it on top of their heads in elaborate styles. Men and women wore the same outfit. It was simply a square of cloth held together with brooches.

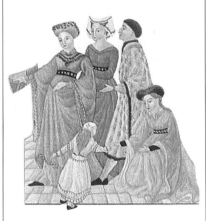

In the Middle Ages
both men and women wore hose. They were like tights and were made of wool or silk, depending on how rich the person was. Later in the Middle Ages, soles were worn to protect the hose.

Men have been wearing tights for several centuries.

This Egyptian woman is putting on her make-up.
On her dressing table are a mirror, make-up boxes and pots of cream.
Both men and women wore a lot of eye-liner. This black sticky liquid they called kohl helped to protect their eyes from the sun's glare.

Getting ready to go out
Up to quite recently people hardly ever washed at all!
Doctors said water carried lots of diseases, so people rarely had baths.
Yet rich people still needed a long time to get ready: having their hair done, putting on their perfume and make-up, dressing in their refined and complicated clothes.

People have been making glass for 4000 years.
Inside the pyramids built by the Ancient Egyptians, archaeologists have discovered glass beads, cups and flasks. But glass was rare, expensive and opaque. Transparent glass was almost unknown until Roman times.

Windows of the past
Have you ever noticed that there aren't any windows in castle walls, just a few narrow slits. Archers could fire through them without being seen while protected from enemy fire.

In the Middle Ages children could play ball without worrying about smashing windows. There were not many windows, which made the houses quite dark. Instead of glass panes, some windows had waxed paper or just curtains – many had nothing at all.

It wasn't until the end of the Middle Ages that glass began to appear more in windows.

■ Quiz

The answers are at the bottom of the next page.

1. What did prehistoric people paint on the walls of caves?
a. the animals they hunted
b. their settlement
c. portraits of people in the tribe

2. What were the pyramids?
a. tombs
b. temples
c. palaces

3. In which city is the Parthenon?
a. Rome
b. Athens
c. London

4. Who built the first road network?
a. the Romans
b. the Egyptians
c. the Franks

5. Who were the Huns?
a. a nation of shepherds
b. a prehistoric tribe
c. barbarian warriors

6. What is parchment made from?
a. very strong paper
b. the leaves of a plant
c. cured sheepskin

7. What did the merchants of the Renaissance buy in the East?
a. potatoes
b. spices and silk
c. cannons

8. What is a bishop's church called?
a. a cathedral
b. a basilica
c. an abbey

9. What did Johannes Gutenberg invent?
a. the cannon
b. the printing press
c. the telegraph

10. Who is America named after?
a. a scientist
b. a printer
c. an explorer

11. Which king was called the Sun King?
a. Francis I
b. Louis XIV
c. Charles V

12. Who built the first train?
a. James Watt
b. George Stephenson
c. Louis Pasteur

■ True or false?

Are these statements true or false?
The answers are at the bottom of the page.

1. Versailles was fitted with electric lighting during Louis XIV's reign.

2. Charlemagne and Julius Caesar met a number of times.

3. The Egyptians worshipped their cats as if they were gods.

4. In the Middle Ages people ate soup for breakfast.

5. It was generally warmer in prehistoric times than it is today.

6. The first cannons were made at the end of the Middle Ages. They mostly just scared enemy soldiers and their horses.

7. The Gauls liked to eat potatoes.

■ Did you know?

Christopher Columbus discovered America in 1492.
On his first visit in 1451, he reached the island of Hispaniola (now called Santo Domingo). On his third expedition he landed in Brazil, on the American continent.
In 1507, the Italian navigator Amerigo Vespucci reached Brazil. Because the map-makers of his time thought he had been the first to reach the new continent, it was called America after him.

How is steel made?
First iron ore is smelted together with coke, a kind of coal. The temperature has to reach at least 2,000 degrees Celsius, which is very hot indeed! The mixture produced is called cast iron and is very brittle. It is heated again so that all the dirt is removed: it has become steel.

Answers:

Quiz
1a, 2a, 3b, 4a, 5c, 6c, 7b, 8a, 9b, 10c, 11b, 12b

True or false
1. False. Electricity wasn't available until the 19th century.
2. False. They lived at different times.
3. True. They embalmed their cats when they died and mummified them.
4. True. They didn't have coffee, tea or chocolate.
5. False. It was colder much of the time.
6. True. They were so primitive that they wounded the soldiers who fired them more often than those they were aiming at.
7. False. Potatoes weren't known in Europe until the 17th century.

■ Fun and games once upon a time

What did children play with in prehistoric times?
Their parents probably made them toys out of wood, bone or leather. But none of these materials last very long and archaeologists haven't found any traces of early toys.

Egyptian children
played with wooden toys, like tops, balls and animals with moving parts. Many have been found in children's tombs.

Children have played the same games throughout history.
Racing, mock fights and ball games have always been favourites.

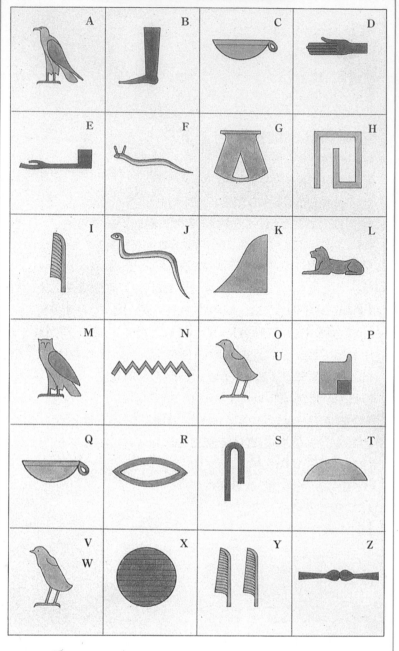

■ Egyptian writing

The Egyptians wrote in hieroglyphs, pictures of objects, animals and plants, which they carved or painted on to the walls of their temples, or on the pedestals of statues.
No one could understand what the hieroglyphs meant, until in the 19th century a French archaeologist, Jean-François Champollion, managed to work out what they said.
There were at least 700 hieroglyphs, including one for each letter of the alphabet.

Grown-ups played quieter games.
They had dice, and board games, like draughts and chess. Cards had been invented by the Chinese. Before being made of cardboard or plastic, they were of ivory or bone.

In hieroglyphic writing a male or female figure was drawn at the end of a name to show whether the person was male or female.

Card and dice games were always very lively, with people betting money on whether the players were going to win or lose.

Chess comes from India. It was introduced into Europe at the beginning of the Middle Ages by the Arabs, when they conquered Spain. In the early days only princes and nobles learned to play chess.

■ Fun and games once upon a time

In the Middle Ages, the Lords' daughters played with rag dolls, which had wax or wooden heads. Their elder brothers played war games with wooden swords. As they got older they began to train to fight in tournaments. They practised against straw dummies.

Jesters and bear-trainers travelled from castle to castle and from village to village entertaining people.

If you had lived at Louis XIV's court you would have played with paper kites, and thrown darts at cork targets. You might have been allowed to watch the courtiers playing chess or cards. And if you were really lucky, the king might have let you watch him play a game of real tennis.

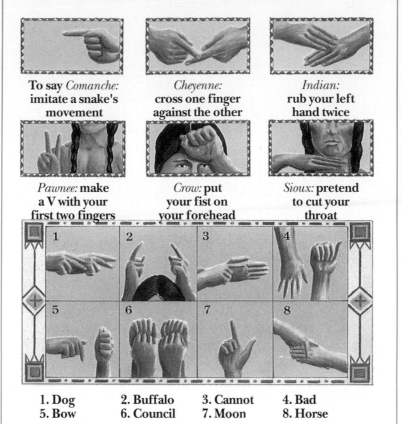

To say *Comanche:* **imitate a snake's movement**

Cheyenne: **cross one finger against the other**

Indian: **rub your left hand twice**

Pawnee: **make a V with your first two fingers**

Crow: **put your fist on your forehead**

Sioux: **pretend to cut your throat**

1. Dog   2. Buffalo   3. Cannot   4. Bad
5. Bow   6. Council   7. Moon   8. Horse

Hands, movements and face painting all meant different things.

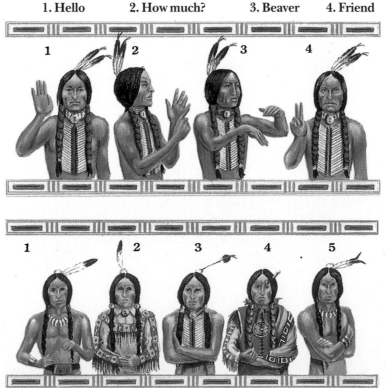

1. Hello   2. How much?   3. Beaver   4. Friend

Arm positions had meanings: 1. Has touched an enemy 2. Has killed with his hands 3. Has found the enemy 4. Has killed with a rifle 5. Has been wounded often

■ Languages without words

Learn the sign language of the native Americans.

Has killed an enemy

War paint

Asking the spirits to send rain...

...or a storm and thunder

The American Indian tribes who lived on the plains all spoke different languages. In order to understand each other they invented a sign language which even the whites learned in the end.

Samuel Morse's 'talking wire'
That's what the native Americans called the electric telegraph which Morse invented in 1844. Messages of dots and dashes were transmitted along a wire, across great distances. They were deciphered with the help of a code, now known as the Morse code.

■ Glossary

Abbot: the head of an abbey or monastery, where monks lived. The head of a women's convent, where nuns lived, was called the abbess.

Christ: Jesus was a Jew, born in Judea when it was a Roman colony. At the age of thirty he began to preach to his people, telling them he was the Son of God. He was crucified in A.D. 33.

Christianity: the religion which follows the teachings of Jesus Christ. After Jesus'death, his followers continued to spread his word throughout the Roman Empire. Over hundreds of years Christianity developed into a European and then a world religion.

Chronology: the order in which events took place in time.

Citizen: in Antiquity, a citizen was the inhabitant of a city.

Colony: an area of land controlled from another country. It may have been won by war and is often settled by people from the invading country.

Constitution: the body of laws and principles by which a country is governed.

Conversion: change to a new or different faith or belief.

Democracy: government by the people or by their chosen representatives.

Gladiator: an armed fighter of ancient Rome who was set against wild animals or other gladiators in the circus.

Guild: an association of businessmen or skilled workers of the Middle Ages.

Hominid: describes all members of the Hominidae family, which includes our prehistoric ancestors as well as ourselves.

Julius Caesar: conquered Gaul in 498 B.C. and invaded England. However England didn't become a Roman colony until after his death in A.D. 43

Missionary: someone who goes abroad to spread his own faith.

Monarchy: a state ruled over by a king or queen.

Nation: a group of people under one government.

Nomad: a member of a tribe or group which is constantly on the move and never settles long in one place.

Oracle: a place where people consult with the gods and ask their advice about the future. In ancient Greece this was usually a temple, where the priests were said to communicate with the gods.

Philosophy: the study of the nature and meaning of existence, reality and goodness. The Greeks were the first to develop philosophy.

Pilgrim Fathers: the English settlers who travelled to America on *The Mayflower* in 1620. They left England because they were not allowed to practise their religion.

Pioneers: people who are among the first to go somewhere or to do something.

Prehistory: the period before written records.

Pope: the head and leader of the Roman Catholic Church. Until the 16th century the Christian church was united and the pope ruled it from Rome.

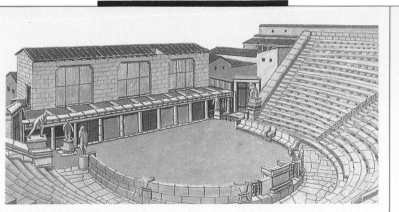

Prospector: someone who looks for gold or any other precious substance found in the ground.

Religion: a system of belief and worship which usually recognizes that there is a power stronger than human beings.

Republic: a state governed by elected representatives. The head of state is not a monarch.

Revolution: the word means full circle and is used to describe a complete change. The French Revolution

saw a total upheaval of beliefs, education, law and the organization of society. The Industrial Revolution in Britain began in the early 19th century: major social changes came as a result of new technologies.

Technology: applications of science to practical things, such as machines.

Vikings: Seafaring Scandinavian tribes who raided the coasts and rivers of Europe, from the 8th century. The Normans (Norsemen) conquered England in 1066.

Here is a list of museums and historical sites you can visit.
But wherever you live, wherever you go, keep your eyes open
and you'll realize how much of the past is around you to see.
Your local library can give you information about historical sites
near you.

Ashmolean Museum
Beaumont Street
Oxford

British Museum
Great Russell Street
London

Fishbourne Roman Palace
West Sussex

Hadrian's Wall
can be seen at: Bardon Mill,
Chester, Corbridge and
Housesteads

Jorvic Viking Centre
York

Museum of London
London Wall
London

National Museum
of Antiquities
of Scotland
Queen Street
Edinburgh

National Museum
of Welsh Antiquities
University College
of North Wales
Bangor

Pitt Rivers Museum
Parks Road
Oxford

Roman Baths
and Pump Room
Stall Street
Bath

Stonehenge
Amesbury
Wiltshire

Ulster Museum
Botanic Gardens
Belfast

Victoria and Albert
Museum
Cromwell Road
London SW7

In Canada:

Canadian Museum
of Civilisation
100 Laurier Street
PO Box 3100
Station B
Hull
Quebec
J8X 4H2

Provincial Museum
of Alberta
12845 - 102nd Avenue
Edmonton
Alberta
T5N 0M6

Royal British Columbia
Museum
675 Belleville Street
Victoria
British Columbia
V8V 1X4

Royal Ontario Museum
100 Queens Park
Toronto
Ontario
M5S 2C6

In Australia:

Australian Museums
6-8 College Street
Sydney NSW 2000

Nicholson Museum
of Antiquities
University of Sydney
Sydney NSW 2006

Museum of Victoria
304-328 Swanston Street
Melbourne VIC 3000

West Australia Museum
Francis Street
Perth WA 6000

INDEX

The entries in **bold** refer to whole chapters on the subject.